Expressions Of Grace

Poetry Collection by
Janiel E. Youngblood

Copyright © 2021 B Radiant LLC

All rights reserved.

ISBN: 978-1-7351766-2-8

Dedication

This work is a testament to my faith, struggles, victories, and lessons learned. It is also a tribute to the many people who have journeyed with me, prayed for me, strengthened me, and guided me which has empowered me to do the same.

Robert, Jayla, and Josalyn, thank you for your love and patience.

Here's to making "**SOME** day" and "**ONE** day" **TODAY**!

Original Artwork by: Josalyn Youngblood

Lighthouse

Traffic signal of the sea,

Lord that's how I want you to use me

A guide through turbulent waves of life's uncertainty

A beacon of light to shine hope in the face of adversity

An extension of your mouth to speak words of truth and encouragement

An extension of your hand to guide and lift from bewilderment

Let the flaws of my weakness make way for your power to fill the space

And let the words of my heart be an expression of your grace

Table of CONTENTS

EXPRESSIONS OF GODLY AFFIRMATION	1
Birthday Blessing	2
You Are My Life, Lord!	4
I Am the Climax of Creation	6
A Masterpiece in Progress	8
The Referral	9
Valentine's Day Message	11
Give Me New Eyes	13
Heed the Warning	14
Thoughts/Reflections	15
EXPRESSIONS OF LOVE	16
For Robert	17
My Why	18
Today and Forever My Love Is Give and Take	20
You are my Sunshine	22
My Favorite Love Song	23
The Priceless Gift	25
Celebrating Marriage	27
Thoughts/Reflections	28
EXPRESSIONS OF INTIMACY	29
Intimacy	30
Missing You	32
Let Me In	33
How's Our Connection	35
Frozen Pipes	36
In That Moment	37
Thoughts/Reflections	38
EXPRESSIONS OF MOTHERHOOD	39
The Ultimate Archeress	40
Your Lifesaving "No"	41
Project Baby Youngblood	43
New Mommy's Prayer	44
Walking Feet	45
Super Mom Saves the Day	47

Thoughts/Reflections	49
EXPRESSIONS OF LOSS	**50**
Gone But Not Forgotten	51
I'm Ready to Go Upstairs	52
Cloud Nine	54
Thank You & Farewell	55
Thoughts/Reflections	57
EXPRESSIONS OF GRATITUDE	**58**
Let Me Be Me	59
The Minority Race	60
Biker Dad's Prayer	61
My Sister Girl, My Friend	62
Teacher Appreciation	63
Tribute to Veterans	64
Reflection on Independence Day	66
Running My Race	67
Actions Speak	69
Lottery	70
Black History Maker	72
Thoughts/Reflections	73

Expressions of Godly Affirmation

Birthday Blessing

As I go into my 40s

I feel like God is saying for me to let Him be

My bodyguard or secret service agent

When I go into new space

He can scan it

Assess all the bullets lined up to take me out

He can protect and shield me

From all the enemies that want to get at me

He wants nothing more than for me to prosper

Why, what's in it for Him?

Me!

He's got my back

My success is His success

My victory is His victory

I can't do this on my own

I desire to be more of a strategic thinker

He lets me know that

He will be the one to give me the strategies

He will be the eyes and ears for me

Sensing all that's going on around me and help me to navigate

I must remove all the noise and distractions

To listen intently to the instructions that He's giving me

It's a life-and-death situation

I must be sensitive to His voice

For His direction for the rest of my life

You Are My Life, Lord!

You Are My Life-lord!

A landlord is one who is the owner of a property

He takes care of the property and has sole responsibility for the property

He chooses a renter and makes a lease agreement with them

As long as they are faithful in paying their rent

Doing their part to keep the property in good condition

He will do his part to maintain the property

When things break or go wrong

The renter has the right to call on the landlord to fix things

God, I am glad that you are my life-lord

You have sole responsibility over my life

You have made an agreement with me in your Word

You will take care of me if I am faithful to you

When things are broken in my life or go wrong

I am glad that I have the right to call on you to fix them

You own my life and know what's necessary to maintain it

Help me to faithfully pay you what I owe you, my tithes and offering, my praise, my time of prayer and devotion

I never want to be late or evicted from your presence

I would not want a life-lord nor a life, Lord, other than with you.

You are the only one who knows how to maintain this property properly

I Am the Climax of Creation

I am the climax of creation, a true work of art so divine

I am the climax of creation, the grand finale to the beginning of time

He set the stage for me

Prepared the place for me

With the bright sun to shine by day

And the moonlight to guide my way

As I walk through the flourishing fields

The trees that so lovely yield

The fruit that becomes my daily bread

Bathe myself by the ocean bed

Yes

He adorned this place for me with the beasts of the field

Lions, tigers, and bears

He filled the sea with fish

The birds to fly in the air

He even had a man awaiting me

I could show up without a single care

He had it all awaiting my arrival

My welcome party was in place

All I had to do was show up on the scene

Designed and fashioned with His amazing grace

I am the climax of creation, a true work of art so divine

I am the climax of creation

The grand finale to the beginning of time

A Masterpiece in Progress

No, he's not perfect but he's off to a good start

He has the spirit of David

He's a man after God's own heart

A master's original

One of a kind

A rare treasure

A work divine

He is of his Father's handiwork continually improving

When you look at his transition

Its evidence the Holy Spirit is moving

Ever evolving in his greatness

He is a fine example of God's faithfulness

Who is this man that has overcome so much

A man whose life has been changed by just one touch

Not just any touch but only through the Lord above

Who has taught him how to be a man through unconditional love

Yes

Truly he is a work of art

He is a man after God's own heart

The Referral

So you say you need a confidant, a therapist

Someone with whom you could discuss your issues

I know exactly what you mean

I've been in your shoes

Let me tell you about my therapist

He's the best I've ever been to

And he works off referrals

So be sure to tell him that I sent you

He's not from around here

He's located in the Pearl Gated Community

His name is Dr. J. Ho Vahnissi

He has an open-door policy

So no pre-scheduled appointment is necessary

He has the best practice in town

With his professional privacy act

You don't have to worry about your business being spread all around

If you become a lifetime member of his services

There are so many rewards

Not only do you get counseling

You get so much more

He offers love, healing, joy, serenity

With a guaranteed reservation to stay at his mansion for eternity

So go ahead

Give him a call

I know that you will be pleased

It's as simple as humbling yourself

And meeting him in prayer on your knees

Valentine's Day Message

I asked God what He wanted to share with you on this Valentine's Day

And in my heart, I believe this is what He wanted to say….

"Every day is Valentine's Day when you have a love like mine

I shower you with my loving kindness all of the time

While others are wooed with chocolates and flowers on one particular day

I'm tickled inside because I give you everything you need each and every day

I shower you not only with the material things that this world provides

The most important of things

I give to you consistently

Money can never buy

No physical touch can compare to feeling of my embrace

No other place where you'll feel so much comfort other than seeking my face

And even in your singleness I have made you completely whole

For my love will never fade away

I am the lover of your soul.

So there is a gift we can give today as part of a special exchange

Even though to the common man it may seem a little strange

But I wish that you'd vow to love yourself for who I have made you to be

And present yourself to me a living sacrifice acceptable and holy

And in return I've done the same in presenting myself totally

I proved my irrevocable love for you by dying on Calvary"

Give Me New Eyes

Give me new eyes God in the face of adversity

Give me new eyes so that I can see my victory

Give me new eyes so that I can see what you see

Give me new eyes that can see pass those things that are faulty in me

Give me new eyes so that I can see clearly, I want to see a new me, a reflection of your glory

Give me new eyes God, so I can see others the through eyes like you

Give me new eyes so that I don't only focus on the wrong that they do

Give me new eyes so I can see hope in the face of despair, the ones that I have are too focused on trouble that's why I need a new pair

Give me new eyes so I can see with love and compassion

Give me new eyes, new sight, new vision

Give me new eyes that see through the tears, see through the dark, and focus on light

Give me new eyes so I can see the manifestation of your Word in my life

Heed the Warning

Don't go back keep moving straight ahead

Don't go back or you could end up dead

Spiritually, emotionally, and maybe physically too

Don't go back 'cause there are too many blessings in store for you

Don't go back to the past from which you came

When you lived a life of guilt, misery, and shame

Press towards the mark for the prize of the high calling

Get deeper in God's Word and He will prevent you from falling

Don't go back to the sin that used to bind

You've grown so much, you've come so far, don't waste your time

You're better, wiser, and so much stronger

The devil can't use his old tricks any longer

So, don't go back keep moving straight ahead

Don't go back or you could end up dead

Spiritually, emotionally, and maybe physically too

Don't go back 'cause there are too many blessings in store for you

Thoughts/Reflections

Expressions of Love

For Robert

R emember that I love you

O ver and over again each day

B elieving in your dreams

E very step of the way

R ight by your side I will always be

T hrough ministering angels watching over thee.

My Why

This prose started as a question but being that you despise any likeness of interrogation

I decided to make it a statement, an exclamation!

The thought came to me of "Why"

In business it's so vital to serve as our guide

It's the driving force for the reason we build when times get rough

It's the dream that keeps us going when going gets tough

So I pondered on the reason of why

Why was I chosen for you to love me?

What's the driving force that makes you stick so closely?

What's the reason that you chose to build with me?

What's getting us through when it's not so easy?

As I stated I'll give my own reply

The deepest answers to the question why

The why of my acceptance to be your bride

The reason I accepted to take this ride

A journey of marital bliss

I'll explain my why for all of this

There's so much about you that is too complex, to limit just to the English language

But if I had to find a few choice words, this is what I'd manage

My why for loving you has to do with a spiritual attraction

More than I at times can even fathom

What is the root cause of the passion within?

It can only be explained as coming from Him

The divine match maker that allowed our destinies to cross

Before you I was completely lost

You are my guide, my navigator to freedom

Freedom in my soul, in my heart, and in my mind

You're the only one that I can see loving until the end of time

Why, because you are the external extension of my soul

You are my other whole

You are the complete individual that embodies the passions I have inside

With you in my life, I have regained a healthy sense of pride

When I look only in your eyes

I see the bright future that God has promised me

You are the vital link to help me reach my God given destiny

We are equally opposite, a match, a perfect fit

You are the male me and the only male for me

No one could ever separate us no matter how hard they try

Chromosomally speaking, I am your X, and you are my Y

Today and Forever My Love Is Give and Take

Today I take your hand in holy matrimony

Today I take a vow to love, honor, and obey you as my one and only

Today I take responsibility to provide a refuge for you to come home to

Today I take pride in knowing the great future that you and God will lead me through

Today I take you in my life as my provider, protector, and king

Today I take you as my head and I being the neck to hold you up above everything

Today I take the first step into the first day of the rest of my life

Today I take your name and proudly become your wife

And in return

I give to you this day my hand in holy matrimony

I give to you this day my love reserved for you only

I give to you this day my body to pleasure as you please

I give to you this day my commitment to fulfill your needs

I give to you this day my devotion and loyalty

I give to you forever my promise of fidelity

I give to you this day a hope for a wonderful future

I give to you this day an opportunity to one day make me a mother that will nurture

I give to you this day me as your crown being that you are my royal king

Today I give you my all as I give you this wedding ring

You are my Sunshine

The sun is always shining even in the darkest night

When we can't see it, we know it's always there

And will resurface with the morning light

I love to feel the warmth of the sun gently kiss my face

And absorb the rays of pleasures all over the place

I find comfort in knowing that behind the clouds of life

There's always sunshine somewhere to make our future bright

Just like the plants need light to remain

Your love is similar and will help us sustain

All the ups and downs that this new journey will bring

You are my guide, my comfort, my best friend through everything

You brighten my world and help me to see

You are my sunshine, that's what you are to me

My Favorite Love Song

Would you like to know my favorite song

The one I could listen to all day long

It's a song that the mockingbird can't sing

A song that's so unique it can't be compared to anything

It's a song with no words or music to hear

Yet it's still a sweet melody in my ear

This song has no notes or even a chorus line

It's just a song you can really feel, after all that is the best kind

And when I say feel, I don't mean it figuratively

I feel this song very literally

So what is this song I love to hear

The rhythmic pattern that penetrates my ear

It's the sound that I hear when I lay my head upon your chest

That steady rhythm that allows me to rest

Safe and secure in your arms

Free of hurt, care, or harm

Yes, this song is greater than any work written even by Mozart

It's the greatest love song ever composed

My favorite song is the sound of your heart….

Oh

Listen

The song has a bridge

Or maybe it's a remix that I didn't notice before

Listen closely

Now that's a sound I can adore

Up until now your heart had a different rhythm than mine

But somehow romantically they're now synchronized in time

Now I know true love has begun

My favorite song now has a harmony

It's the sound of our hearts beating as one

The Priceless Gift

My gift was so awesome

More rich than fine wine

More precious than a gem of any kind

Something that I could claim as all mine

The temperature was so right

The sky was so bright

I held him so tight

Oh the cool breeze through my hair

The affection that we share

How I wanted to stay there

As we read from God's Word

Adoration is what I heard

As he read the 31st of Proverbs

Walking hand in hand

To a light brunch on demand

Chocolate muffin and banana nut bran

Hot chocolate and whipped cream

Then off to hook up my new washing machine

I was so excited that I wanted to scream

Because my gift was so awesome

More rich than fine wine

More precious than a gem of any kind

Something that I could claim as all mine

The priceless gift that I received was the quality of His Time

Celebrating Marriage

Oh what a sweet and exciting time it is on the wedding day

When everyone comes together to wish you well and to say

Congratulations on the bond that was solidified

Festively celebrate the knot that is tied

There's also recognition at anniversary time

Some may stop by to drop you a line

But what about those in between days

When the everyday little victories deserve a little praise

When the daily grind gets in the way

Of all the sweet marital bliss that may seem to have gone astray

I want to encourage you and your spouse

Continue to let an abundance of love fill your house

Keep up the great work of learning and loving each other every day

You never know who you're inspiring along the way

May your marriage continually be strong, and you remain forever a pair

Feeling comforted in knowing that you are in someone's thoughts and prayers

Thoughts/Reflections

Expressions of Intimacy

Intimacy

The distance between us grows with each passing day

There is so much that I want to share with you

So much I have to say

I do nice things for you, hoping that you'll notice me

Though I don't want your obligation

I want you to want my intimacy

I prepare your food each day

A nice place for you to come home to

I only want so much to be close to you

But often I hear you say you're busy with work and other important tasks

Just a little intimacy more frequently is all that I ask

The few times that we do come together, it's a little "quicky"

Only you are satisfied

I wish for the moments to last longer so that I too can be gratified

It seems you only come to me when it's something you desire badly

But what about my needs to be fulfilled and express my love to you madly

How can you resist me?

My praises, don't you want to sing?

After all, I am your creator, it is me who has blessed you with everything

For I am your groom, and you are my bride

It is for your life that I became flesh to die

Seek me now and always is my earnest plea

You can have the desires of your heart when you give me intimacy

Missing You

You ever been in a crowd, yet still feel all alone?

Ever been in a loving relationship, yet still feel unloved?

How about having thoughts of why doesn't he want me as much as I want him?

Why in those quiet moments

Right before he goes to sleep

Doesn't he think of me

And display that gesture with a call?

Why am I not the thing that excites him and what he's most passionate about?

Why would he rather be out with his friends than spend quality time with me?

Initially we had momentum

I was sure that our relationship was tighter than any other

I had his undivided attention, after all we were best friends

Where did I go wrong?

I gave all I had

I even died for his sins

Let Me In

Don't build up a wall and not let me in

Don't build a fortress around your emotions and exclude your best friend

Let me into your heart, your emotions, and mind

Let me understand you, your uniqueness, your rare kind

If you are frustrated, I'll pray for clarity

If you're feeling pressured by the stresses of life, I'll pray for release

But just let me know your need and I'll take it to the Lord above

It would be my honor and the sincerest expression of my love

I know I must digress and respect your space

Although it's difficult to see unhappiness on your face

I desire to know where it hurts so I can apply the bandage of my love and care

Is it here in the relationship, there in the pockets, or does it seem like everywhere

Okay, okay I won't nag anymore

Just know that I'm always here for you and my heart and ears are like an open door.

So whenever you want to talk, I'm ready to listen and learn

To be drawn closer to you is what I yearn

We are one flesh so you're never alone in your fight

The Word says that one can take a thousand but two send ten thousand to flight

We serve such an awesome God, any burden He can bare.

Know that He and I both love you dearly and will always be right there

How's Our Connection

Caller can you hear me now?

What's the disruption that's hindering the sound?

Did we hit a dead zone

Where we both feel like we're talking alone?

Is there static in the way

That's hindering what we want to say?

We don't need a new model or new contract

Perhaps a system upgrade

Restore the default settings

Get the connection back

I just want to hear your heart

For you to hear mine

Nothing in the way

Clogging the proverbial line

It's best for us to stand closer to the Tower

That's where we get the power

We must remove all background sound

So finally we can affirmatively reply when asked

Caller can you hear me now?

Frozen Pipes

It's wintertime and the pipes are frozen

It's a consequence to the thing you've chosen

Didn't momma ever tell you to keep a constant flow

It's not until the flow stops that you remember what you know

Even a little bit a little often is what you ought to do

But when you let it go too long there ain't nothing coming through

So now you have to wait it out until this season has passed

And be respectful of the flow and you'll get it when you ask

But for now, its wintertime and the pipes are frozen

It's the consequence to the things you've chosen

In That Moment

In that moment

Our hearts are beating as one

Reflecting on how far we've come

Past battles we've won

In that moment

I don't have a care in the world

Not even focused on the girls

In that moment

I'm not concerned about bills that are due

In that moment

It's all about me and you

In that moment

There's no telling where my body ends

Where yours begin

I want that moment to last forever

As if time had no end

In that moment

I feel a sense of security

In that moment

I thank God for giving you to me

Thoughts/Reflections

Expressions of Motherhood

The Ultimate Archeress

My mother has often referred to her children as arrows being shot forth according to Psalms 127:4

If her children are the arrows, then she is the Ultimate Archeress. She has shot forth her children using Godly wisdom even though she was too young to have the bow.

She ensured that her children were surrounded by people who could help guide her arrows in the right direction.

Through prayer, fighting in the spirit, as well as in the natural at times, she has made sure that her children hit their intended target.

Not only has she been the person to shoot forth arrows of her own, but God has also used her to help direct the arrows of others, as she has been like a mother to many.

She is gifted in areas other than archery too.

This is a woman who can recreate almost anything with her hands, can stretch a dollar to provide for her family, braid any head with the least amount of hair, make thrift store apparel look like high priced fashion, listen over the phone to a car that won't turn over and diagnose a solution, and she can sure enough pray one man out of her daughter's life and pray the right one in.

This is surely a woman worth celebrating.

I'm proud to call her Mommy!

Your Lifesaving "No"

Thank you for saying "No" to sleeping in your bed at night

This taught me to deal with my fears, and face my frights

Thanks for saying "No" to keeping the money we found at the bank we used to clean

This taught me that integrity is doing the right thing even when you think you're not being seen

Thanks for saying "No" to me going out with friends you didn't know

Your intuition proved to be right as we watched those so-called friends grow

Thanks for saying "No" to the parties that I thought would be so much fun

You made up for it by the annual trip with family and friends to Wild Water Kingdom

Thanks for saying "No" when I wanted skip church for activities, and you just wouldn't bend

Only to find later that I would end up playing church in the garage with my friends

Thanks for saying "No" to passivity and being bold about what you had to say

You were often the mama bear or a loud roaring lioness that would literally run the mean kids away

I know your hardest "No" had to be the disagreement in what I thought was love

But you standing firm taught me to hold true as a mother to the promises from God above

For every "No", I can count a hundred "Yeses"

As you always pushed me to be the very best

Your "No's" have shaped my life in such a remarkable way

Such that all these years later I can look to you with deep sincerity and say

"Thank you Mom, I appreciate and love you so much

I celebrate you today!"

Project Baby Youngblood

Finally, it's time to put my plans into action

I've had these blueprints since the beginning of all creation

Waiting for such a time as this

When I could bless a couple with a special kind of bliss

Ok team, it's time to go to work

We've got a special project on our hands

We've only got 40 weeks to bring it to completion

So every minute counts to meet our demand

Double check all systems to ensure they're working exactly to the manufacturer's design

Go easy on the carrier, this will be her first time

Now it's more than just the standard model

The owners have requested an upgrade

Healthy, obedient, and saved at an early age

Although we must work tirelessly

It will all be worth it in the end

Because at the unveiling ceremony

We shall receive all praises from the owners, their family and friends

I get so excited to have the task of manifesting my love

When we have fully completed the making of Baby Youngblood

New Mommy's Prayer

This new life growing inside of me

You've equipped me to guide its destiny

Awesome blessings yet to be told

The joy of watching my baby grow old

There's no comparable feeling I can explain

The essence of love that is contained

In my womb but attached to my heart

The bond between mother and child that shall never part

You've blessed me indeed to carry the seed through

What my child shall become is my gift back to you

Walking Feet

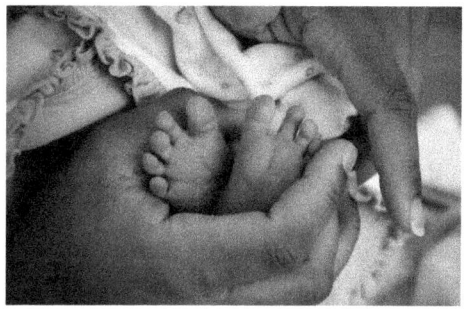

Those little feet that use to kick inside my womb

Creating ripples across my belly as you ran out of room

Feet that I would kiss so soft and sweetly

Tickle to get you to flash that cute smile at me

Feet that I could hold together and still fit in one hand

Are now the feet that make you strong enough to stand

All by yourself now wow you're growing up

Now I am able to let go, offering only a slight touch

Cause those cute little tootsies are now walking feet

Feet that you'll use as I closely watch you cross the street

They may be used to dance across Broadway's stage or run down a basketball court

Could be a soccer field, baseball diamond, or some other sport

They may lead you down a run-away in fashion model style

Could be a court room, hospital hall, and maybe a wedding aisle

I pray that they carry you through life until an age very old

But most importantly my mission is to guarantee

They walk you on the streets of gold

Super Mom Saves the Day

Her skills are great but may only be recognized by few

She is the most significant resource because of all she can do

She may not realize her true worth

But her value is high

If the resume were written, no one could deny

All the roles this one woman has to play

Many simultaneously or all in one day

Nurse, Teacher, Provider, and Protector

Chef, Beautician, Fashion Designer, and Finance Director

Judge, Lawyer, and sometimes even Prosecutor

Monster Slayer right before its time to go to bed

Thermometer who can detect a fever by the touch of the head

Storyteller and Singer of sweet lullabies

Referee over fighting siblings

Disciplinary, Detector of Lies

Project Manager, Organizer and Taxicab Driver

Counselor, Consoler, Interpreter and Problem Solver

Repair Woman, Stain Remover, and Housekeeper

Cheerleader, Photographer, and Personal Shopper

Track Star when she keeps a running toddler from harm

Seatbelt Reinforcer with the extension of the right arm

For her children, these are some of the hats that a good mother must wear

It's all part of the responsibility that God equipped her to bear

She can rely on His Strength when her own seems low

After all, they are His seed, she just has the pleasure of helping them grow

Thoughts/Reflections

Expressions of Loss

Gone But Not Forgotten

I have heard it said that it's better to have loved and lost

Then to have never experienced love at all

While those words may be true

Even a year later, the pain is still raw

Giving birth is a unique experience

To have a living extension of you disconnected and apart

The baby is and forever will be very much attached to your heart

In time the pain will lessen

Memories and love will never fade away

Your precious baby is not gone forever

She's just waiting in Heaven to be reunited with you one day

I'm Ready to Go Upstairs

Inspired by the last words of Pricilla "Nanny" Gilbert

I'm ready to go upstairs now

To see my master that sits on high

I'm ready to go upstairs now

To my mansion in the sky

I'm ready to go upstairs now

No more pain to endure

I'm ready to go upstairs now

Where I can rest for sure

I'm ready to go upstairs now

To see my Lord face to face

I'm ready to go upstairs now

To thank Him for His saving grace

I'm ready to go upstairs now

To see the people I love so dear

I'm ready to go upstairs now

I'll be waiting for you when you get there

Cloud Nine

I now know why it's called Cloud Nine

The spot that resonates way high in the sky

Well I should say temporarily resonates

In thin air to easily dissipate

No surface on which to securely stand

No substance to handle relationships' demands

When the storms come, darkness quickly appears

Cloud Nine then holds the water that soon become tears

That fall like rain back to the ground

Reality sets in and that's where feelings are now found

Not in the sky anymore but on something more secure

Come to grips with yourself and be more mature

Although there's some security in the hardness

Feelings like to roam

Gravitating back to the sky

Yearning for Cloud Nine to become home

Thank You & Farewell

Thank you for allowing me to love

Even though you weren't worthy of the love I had to give

But what the experience proved to me was

I am capable of loving deeply, unconditionally, in spite of, because of, forsaking all others too

They say love is blind, but it's deaf and dumb as well

But it's okay, you live, you love, you learn

Yet and still, I thank you

Because of you, I now recognize deceit and
I've learned to trust my intuition

Because of you, I know what hurt is and healing too

But I'm thankful most of all for the maturity I see in me that's led me to my destiny

I can now love freely, and give myself to a man that's worthy, who's full of chivalry and proves his love for me daily

Unlike you, he faithfully commits to me unconditionally

So I bid you farewell

You no longer have a place in my life, my heart, or my mind

The hurt is healed, no bitterness remains

I release you, as the bind that tied our souls together is destroyed

I am free

Free to move pass the past and rejoice about my future

For you were the dark night that had to come before my sunshine

My future is much brighter now since I have awakened to a brand-new day

Thoughts/Reflections

Expressions of Gratitude

Let Me Be Me

Who are they trying to make me be?

Why can't I just be me?

Grow at my own pace

Be confident in my own space

Just let me be

Love me for me

Can I be free?

Free to be me

I'm tired of trying to be something that I'm not

To please others that I can not

Like it or leave it

Work with it or around it

That's how you found it

Be patient with it

It is who I am

I will grow and change but until then

Just let me be

The Minority Race

He has become a minority

Not by chance but by choice

He has been separated by the majority

Can't you tell by the sound of his voice

He could be considered a victim of society

Not because of the color of his skin

But it's because of the series of positive decisions

That he's made within

He's often talked about, ridiculed

Even stabbed in his back

It's because he has something the majority lacks

But he's no victim he's a victor

Because truth and honesty guide his feet

Unlike the majority

Who comfortably walk in selfishness, lies, and deceit

He is a part of the minority race

Not distinguished by color or ethnicity

He is among the minority

That have character and integrity

Biker Dad's Prayer

Every time I hear an engine rev or see a motorcycle zoom by

I can't help but say a prayer my biker guy

I vividly remember as a little girl

Riding on the bike with him

On that "Thriller" ride with the helmet fastened tightly under my chin

Lord, protect my dad as he travels on his motorcycle day by day

Keep him safe on every single highway, byway, and parkway

As he travels with his crew feeling young and free

Keep your guardian angels encamped all around him and his precious Harley

My Sister Girl, My Friend

So here's a message for you

Cause you've been a friend through and through

This is a special birthday this year and yes, I'll tease

Cause it's the last one you'll celebrate in your twenties

We've been through a lot and I know more is to come

But we've stuck through it all and the years have been fun

We've laughed, we cried

We've celebrated

Endured the lies

We've been through the hair color change,

Address change

Name change too

But one thing that's remained the same

Is the bond between me and you

But overall we've been victorious throughout everything

Cause we are both Daddy's girls

Daughters of the king

So always remember to wear your crown proudly this year

For we know our blessings are on the way

In fact, some are already here

Teacher Appreciation

May God bless you for all that you do

You teach our children and show them so much love too

You are so caring, so patient, so kind

When parents hurry off to work, they have peace of mind

Knowing they leave their precious ones in good hands

With teachers that instruct them well and help them understand

Many early life lessons through scriptures, reading, songs, and art

Partnering with parents to give the children an early start

In the value of education and development of skills

How awesome, humbling, and rewarding it feels

To know that together we are shaping the next generation

Of mathematicians, scientists, and maybe even the President of our nation

For your significant work

I thank you again

May you reap a great return for your investment in our children

Tribute to Veterans

Your service is not forgotten

Your bravery is still worth praising

Because of your courage

There is hope for the children that I am now raising

You were willing to sacrifice it all for our country, our homeland

Despite the differences that exist

When it comes to protecting our freedom,

United We Stand

So I honor you today in appreciation

For your sacrifice and willingness to selflessly serve

May God open the windows of Heaven

May God grant you all the many blessings you deserve

As you are now a freedom fighter in the Lord's army

You are a faithful soldier

Using spiritual weapons of warfare to defeat the enemy

You've moved through the ranks

Rallied the troops like a true General Officer of the military

You've equipped new soldiers to fight this good fight of faith

Taught the Word of God with authority

We have an expected end since the war is rigged in our favor

No longer needing guns or grenades

The battle is already won

As we fight with our songs of praise

We are more than conquerors together

I am proud to have warriors like you on the same side as me

We'll continue to stand strong until in Heaven

We have our welcome home parade of Victory

Reflection on Independence Day

This year on Independence Day

I have an interesting proposition

You know there's another kind of Independence

That deserves special recognition

It's the freedom that we have from hell and the devil's oppressive schemes

We are victorious through Jesus Christ if we trust Him and believe

I encourage you to not only think about the signing of that significant document on the Fourth of July

But reflect on the signature with shed blood on the day that Jesus died

Think about more than fireworks, cookouts, and summer fun

But focus on all that the Lord has done

He saved you, delivered you and set you free

That's what Independence Day means to me

Our country was founded on Godly principles

Somehow, we've forgotten that fact

But this year for Independence Day

Let's bring those values back

Let's praise our God for what we've endured in the years of our past

Rejoicing over the fact that we are truly free at last

Running My Race

Oh the joy that fills my soul

When the payment meets my soles

It's no longer about fighting off potential weight gain

It's all about keeping myself mentally sane

The stress relief that comes with every step on the road or sidewalk

Oh the stories to be told if the streets could talk

It's the race against myself for the goal of personal win

My running buddy who applies positive peer pressure

When I'm struggling to end or even begin

It's overcoming the harsh wind and water puddles

When my fingers feel like they'll freeze

Pushing through the thick humidity longing for a cool breeze

It's so worth it when the endorphins flow

I complete my course with that finisher's glow

The Bible says the race is not given to the swift but to the one who endures

Even when my pace is slow

The run refreshes me, restores me

It is anxiety's cure

I'm thankful for my strong body, determined will and willing feet

And all the running warriors that this therapeutic sport has allowed me to meet

Actions Speak

No service is better than just lip service

We must back up what we say

We must be habitual to praise and affirm the Lord

Each and everyday

He's also requiring that we put

Some action behind our words too

Express our love and gratitude

In the things we say and do

Step out and express His love to others

Through kindness and care

Be the hands and mouth of God

Represent him boldly if you dare

When you get up off your knees

That's when the real work begins

Don't just tell him you love Him

But show him you love Him

By working as unto Him

Lottery

I for so long viewed our society

To be one filled with so much negativity

But what has come to my reality

Is the optimism that exist so greatly

Among the millions of people who play the lottery

What this proves to me emphatically

Is that our society is filled with positivity

But it's not dispersed about rationally

You see, many people do seem to think optimistically

But mostly concerning things they cannot control entirely

It's sad to think that people have more faith

When something or someone else is in control

But they are less likely to believe

When they have a chance to play the dominant role

They will gamble and play lotto

When the odds are stacked against them

But won't take a chance to step out

And pursue their dreams in a vehicle where they are sure to win

What have we come to

If people don't even believe in themselves

Setting their hopes and dreams

Desperately on a shelf

Our graveyards are too full

With the best novelists, athletes, ideas, and songs

People have become too numb to the burning passion inside

They have held back way too long

It's time to wake up to the life

That we were meant to live

Leave our mark on this world

While we still have a chance to give

The lottery is too risky

Slots and stock markets too

But true-life fortune is sure to be obtained

If you just take a chance on the dreams inside of you

Black History Maker

Each day that we live

Each day that we give

We are making history

Each day that we strive

To keep the dream alive

We are making history

Through the lives that we touch

Letting others know that they matter so much

We are making history

By the person you are

The many things you've done

You have stepped up to be that one

You are making history

Thoughts/Reflections

www.ingramcontent.com/pod-product-compliance
Lightning Source LLC
Chambersburg PA
CBHW071913070526
44583CB00016B/1974